Contents

Macmillan Education
4 Crinan Street
London N1 9XW
A division of Macmillan Education Limited

Companies and representatives throughout the world

Ferris Wheel Level 2 Student's Book ISBN 978-1-380-01867-0
Ferris Wheel Level 2 Student's Book Pack ISBN 978-1-380-02668-2

First published 2019

Original design by Clare Webber.
Page make-up by emc design ltd.
Illustrated by Jose Ignacio Gômez (Nacho Gômez) pp3–84(all character artwork and main illustrations);
Animation Group Sp. z o.o. pp85-96.
Cover design by emc design ltd.
Cover illustration by Jose Ignacio Gômez (Nacho Gômez).
Picture research by Lorraine Beck.

Author's acknowledgements
I would like to thank everyone at Macmillan Education in the UK, Spain and Mexico who has contributed to the development and production of these materials. I would also like to thank all the teachers who have taken time to read and pilot the materials, and given invaluable feedback at every stage of writing the course. Special thanks as ever go to my husband, Alan, for his encouragement and support, and to our son and daughter, Jamie and Hannah, from whose early childhood days I learnt so much.

The publishers would like to thank Alex Tamulis, São Paulo, Brazil; Ayşegül Sezer, İNO Schools, Turkey; Daniela Araujo Pielli, Alt Idiomas, São Bernardo Do Campo, Brazil; Daniela Pugliese, Milton's College, Buenos Aires, Argentina; Esra Ezici, Turkey; Fernanda Domeniconi Nery Amorim, São Paulo, Brazil; Gabriela Iocolari, English Schoolhouse, Buenos Aires, Argentina; Gulbin Cin, Bahcesehir College, Turkey; Mariana Pastorino, Em Pi Instituto de Inglês, Santa Fe, Argentina; Mariné Ortiz, Warrington, Buenos Aires, Argentina; Paola Daniela Tuninetti, Academia Argüello, Córdoba, Argentina; Silvana Paola Accardo, Escuela Cooperativa Mundo Nuevo Instituto Casa de Jesús, Buenos Aires, Argentina

Printed and bound in Brazil.
2025
49

The author and publishers would like to thank the following for permission to reproduce their images:

Alamy Stock Photo/lee avison p24(pasta), Alamy Stock Photo/Blend Images p11(bmr), Alamy Stock Photo/EyeEm pp75, 76, 83(star), Alamy Stock Photo/Granger Historical Picture Archive pp75, 76, 83(planet), Alamy Stock Photo/Ivan Kmit pp31, 33(trees), Alamy Stock Photo/Fritz Liedtke pp35, 43(living room), Alamy Stock Photo/Radius Images pp75, 76, 83(sun), Alamy Stock Photo/Zoonar GmbH pp25, 33(dress), 65, 69, 73(car); **Getty Images/**3DSculptor p76(rocket), Getty Images/AlexStar p54(l), Getty Images/Alexthq pp25, 32, 33(pants), Getty Images/aluxum pp51, 53(garden), Getty Images/Antagain pp55, 56, 63(hen),Getty Images/ArcaidImages/Diane Auckland pp35, 43(dining room), Getty Images/artpartner-images pp65, 66, 73(plane), Getty Images/Artpilot pp15, 23(legs), Getty Images/baona pp15, 23(tummy), Getty Images/Carolyn Barber pp35, 43(bathroom), Getty Images/CHUYN p71(bmr), Getty Images/David Clapp pp81(r), 83(night sky), Getty Images/cosmonaut p11(bml), Getty Images/Creative Crop pp45, 46, 53(cereal), Getty Images/Dorling Kindersley p32 (shoes), Getty Images/Michael Duva pp55, 56, 63(duck), Getty Images/eurobanks pp5, 6, 13(bag), Getty Images/Fuse pp55, 56, 63(goat), p59(goat insert r), Getty Images/Lenora Gim p41(bl), Getty Images/GlobalP pp55, 56, 61, 63(sheep, cow, dog), pp56, 61(horse), p59(dog, goat insert l), p61(puppy, calf, foal), pp61, 63(lamb), p75(dog, goat insert), p59 Getty Images/Glow Decor pp35, 43(bedroom), Getty Images/Peter Gridley pp75, 83(sky), Getty Images/hadynyah pp71(br), 73(br sky), Getty Images/Hemera Technologies pp6, 74 (paper), Getty Images/hillwoman2 p41(br), Getty Images/hudiemm p51(tomatoes), Getty Images/iStockphoto/DGLimages p11(bl), Getty Images/iStockphoto/sharpshutter pp21, 23(field), Getty Images/iStockphoto/Thinkstock Images/Anson_iStock pp75, 76, 83(moon), Getty Images/j-wildman pp59, 63(farm), Getty Images/Jamakosy pp51, 53(potatoes), Getty Images/Jamesmcq24 pp45, 46, 51, 53(bread), Getty Images/JBryson p11(tmr), Getty Images/JohnnyGreig pp15, 23(arms), Getty Images/kamski pp65, 66, 73(boat), Getty Images/keni1 p11(br), Getty Images/Dave King pp25, 32, 33(coat), 13(br), Getty Images/krungchingpixs pp15, 23(feet), Getty Images/lucielang pp5, 13, 24, 44, 64, 74(crayons), Getty Images/mawielobob pp25, 33(skirt), Getty Images/milanfoto pp46, 51(bananas), Getty Images/moodboard pp15, 23(head), Getty Images/narvikk p56(rooster), Getty Images/Nerthuz pp65, 66, 69, 73(bus), 66(truck), Getty Images/nuiiko pp15, 23(hands), Getty Images/NYS444 pp25, 33(sweater), Getty Images/parinyabinsuk p34(pegs), Getty Images/PeopleImages p11(tr), Getty Images/Per Magnus Persson pp41, 43(toybox), Getty Images/PetrMalyshev pp5, 6, 13(pencil case), Getty Images/PhotoAlto/Laurence Mouton p51(pears), Getty Images/Photodisc p76(astronaut), Getty Images/piovesempre p41(bml), Getty Images/Andrea Pistolesi pp81(l), 83(sky with rainbow), Getty Images/Rawpixel p66(motorcycle), Getty Images/Aigars Reinholds pp25, 32, 33(shirt), Getty Images/Andrea Rugg pp35, 43(kitchen), Getty Images/scanrail pp65, 66, 73(train), Getty Images/Science Photo Library pp46, 51, 53(carrots), Getty Images/Serg_Velusceac pp6, 14, 34, 84(paints), Getty Images/Sergiy1975 pp65, 69, 73(bike), Getty Images/Richard Sharrocks pp5, 6, 13(scissors), Getty Images/SheraleeS p71(bml), Getty Images/Spaces Images p21(climbing frame), Getty Images/STOCK4B/Silas pp35, 43(house), Getty Images/stockcam pp45, 46, 51, 53(eggs), Getty Images/Stocktrek Images pp75, 83(earth), Getty Images/Kutay Tanir p44 (milk carton), Getty Images/Chris Tobin p71(bl), Getty Images/trigga pp45, 46, 51, 53(milk), Getty Images/Tsuji pp45, 46, 51, 53(apples), Getty Images/Udomsook pp5, 13, 14(pencil); **iStockphoto/**alex_kz pp5, 6, 13, 14, 24, 44, 64, 74, 84(glue); **Shutterstock/**Robyn Mackenzie pp51, 53(peas), Shutterstock/M. Unal Ozmen pp45, 46, 53(ice cream); **www.imagesource.com** p34(string).

Commissioned photographs by Helen Marsden/Spectrecom pp7(c), 9, 13(Sam, Anna), 14(c), 15(Anna and Sam), 16(1–3, paper), 19, 21, 25, 27(Anna and Sam), 28(1–3), 31, 33, 37(Anna, Sam), 39(Anna and Sam), 40(1–3), 43, 45, 49(Sam, Anna), 52(1–3), 55(c), 57, 61(c), 63(Anna and Sam), 64(1–3), 67(br), 69, 73(tr), 76(1–3, tissue paper), 79(c), 81, 85(tr), 88(1–3), 91(tr), 93, 97(tr), 100(1–3, tissue paper, stickers); Spectrecom Education Ltd pp11, 14(tr), 23, 26, 35, 38(tl, tc, tr), 47, 50, 51(Anna, Sam and Uncle Dan), 59, 62, 71(Anna and Sam, Uncle Dan), 74, 83(tl), 86, 87(Uncle Dan), 95, 98, 99(Anna, Sam and Uncle Dan).

Hello I'm Mimi!

Listen, point and repeat. Sing *Hello, I'm Mimi*. Stick the color stickers. Color the flag your favorite color. Language: Mommy, Daddy, Mimi, Dylan; Ferris Wheel; blue, green, orange, pink, red, yellow; numbers; Hello, I'm (Mimi).

Lesson 2 Language

1:18

hello

Listen, find and point. Sing *Where's the ball?* Circle the toys. Draw your favorite toy. Ask and say. **Language:** ball, car, doll, scooter, teddy, train; blue, green, orange, pink, red, yellow; Where's the (ball)? Here's the (ball)! It's (blue).

Classroom

Fun with paint!

1:19 hello 1:20

Listen, point and repeat. Listen and play. Stick the classroom object stickers. Circle the classroom objects that you have. Say. Language: backpack, crayons, glue, pencil, pencil case, scissors; blue, green, orange, pink, red, yellow

Listen and find the new classroom objects. Listen, point and sing *Do you have your backpack?* Circle the objects Sam has. Ask and say. Language: backpack, glue, paints, paper, pencil case, scissors; Do you have your (backpack)? Yes, I do. / No, I don't.

Lesson 3 Story

Watch. Listen to the story *Fun with paint!* Circle the classroom objects Dylan uses to do his picture. Stick the story sticker. **Language:** backpack, crayons, glue, paints, paper, pencil, pencil case, scissors; colors; Do you have (paper)? Yes, I do. / No, I don't. I have (red) paint.

Lesson 4 Story Song

Classroom

Watch. Listen, point and sing *The paint song*. Draw a picture of your favorite place. Say the colors in your picture. Say the classroom objects you use.
Language: crayons, glue, paints, pencil, scissors; colors; I have (blue) here.

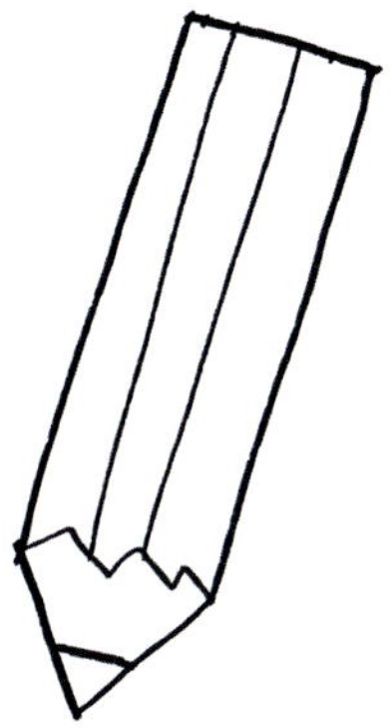

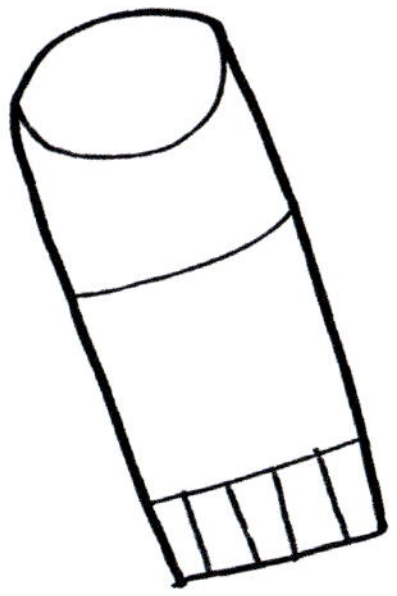

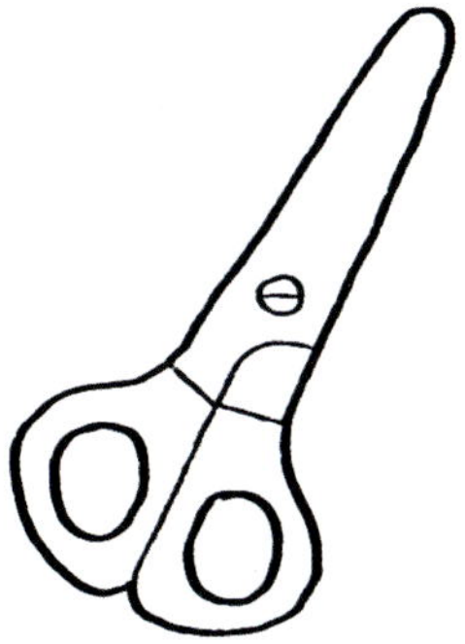

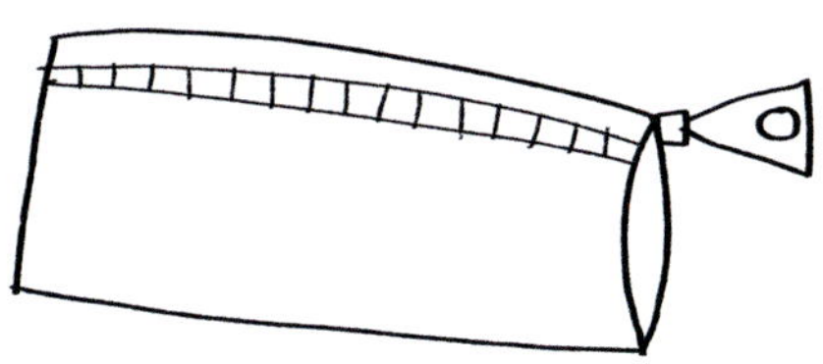

Watch. Listen and point. Circle the objects Uncle Dan has. Color the star if Uncle Dan is ready. Color the objects you have. Ask and say. **Language:** crayons, glue, paints, paper, pencil, pencil case, scissors; Do you have (a pencil)? Yes. / No. I have (paper). I don't have (scissors).

Values Good behavior

Classroom

1:28

hello

Listen, point and sing *Be good at home*. Color the pictures of good behavior.
Draw a picture of you being good at home or school. Say.
Language: home, school; Daddy, Mommy, Teacher; I'm good at (home).

SOCIAL AND EMOTIONAL LEARNING

Lesson 7
Content

1:29

hello

Listen and point. Follow and draw the paths from the children to the places at school. Say the places.
Language: cafeteria, classroom, library, playground; Go to the (playground).

Culture

1:30 hello

Watch. Listen, point and sing *Wind the bobbin up*. Color the ceiling. Say.
Language: ceiling, clap, door, floor, hands, knee, window; Point to the (ceiling).

Review

I can ...

Vocabulary

Story

Speaking

Content

Trace and color the classroom objects you know. Listen, point and say. Ask and say. Complete the faces to show what you can do. Language: backpack, crayons, glue, paints, paper, pencil, pencil case, scissors; Do you have (glue)? Yes, I do. / No, I don't. I have (crayons). I don't have (paints).

Project

COOPERATIVE LEARNING

Name the classroom objects you need. Make the Ferris Wheel. Say the colors. Draw a picture of you to go on the Ferris Wheel. **Language:** Ferris Wheel; crayons, glue, paints, paper, pencil; colors; I have (paints). My wheel is (orange). I'm on (blue). I like the (blue) wheel. Our Ferris Wheel is (fantastic)!

My body
I can dance!

Listen, point and repeat. Listen and play. Stick the body stickers. Circle the parts of the body Mimi and Dylan are moving. Say. Language: arms, feet, hands, head, legs, tummy; blue, green, orange, pink, red, yellow

Listen and find the new parts of the body. Listen, point and sing *I can move my head*.
Draw a picture of you. Say what you can do.
Language: arms, feet, fingers, hands, head, legs, toes, tummy; I can/can't move my (head). Can you?

Lesson 3 Story

1:37

Watch. Listen to the story *I can dance!* Circle who helps Mimi learn to dance. Stick the story sticker. Language: arms, feet, head, legs; Can you move your (head)? Yes, I can. / No, I can't. I can/can't dance. I can/can't move my (arms).

Lesson 4

Story Song

My body

Watch. Listen, point and sing *I can dance. You can dance too.* Match and color. Say. Language: arms, feet, head, legs; Move your (head). I can (dance).

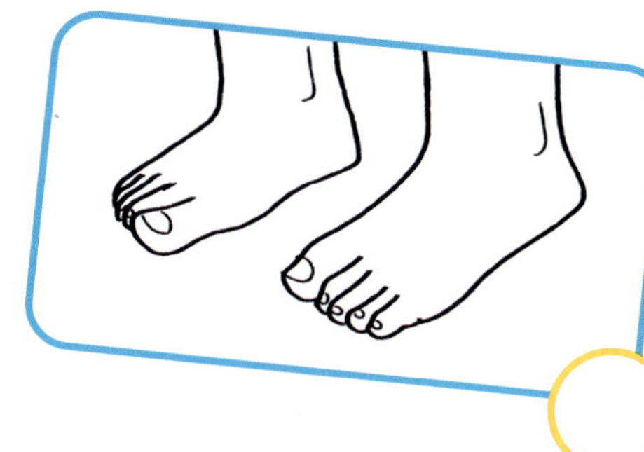

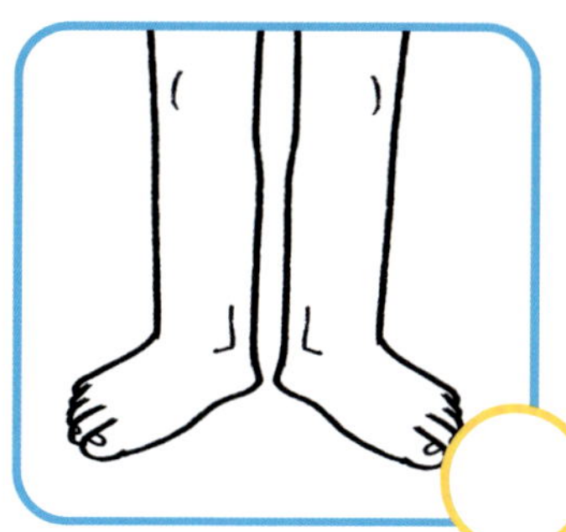

1:40

hello

Watch. Listen and point. Color the circles green to show what Uncle Dan can do and red to show what he can't do. Color the pictures to show what you can do. Ask and say. **Language:** arms, feet, hands, head, legs, tummy; Can you move your (head)? Yes, I can. / No, I can't. What can you do? I can move my (head).

Values Making an effort

Listen, point and sing *I can do it if I try*. Match. Color what you can do if you try. Say. **Language:** coat, scissors, shoes; I can/can't put on my (shoes). I can/can't cut with scissors.

SOCIAL AND EMOTIONAL LEARNING

Listen and point. Trace the ✔ or ✘ to show what Sam and Anna can and can't do. Color the pictures to show what you can do. Ask and say.

Language: climb, hop, jump, run; Can you (run)? Yes, I can. / No, I can't. I can/can't (climb).

Lesson 8

Culture

My body

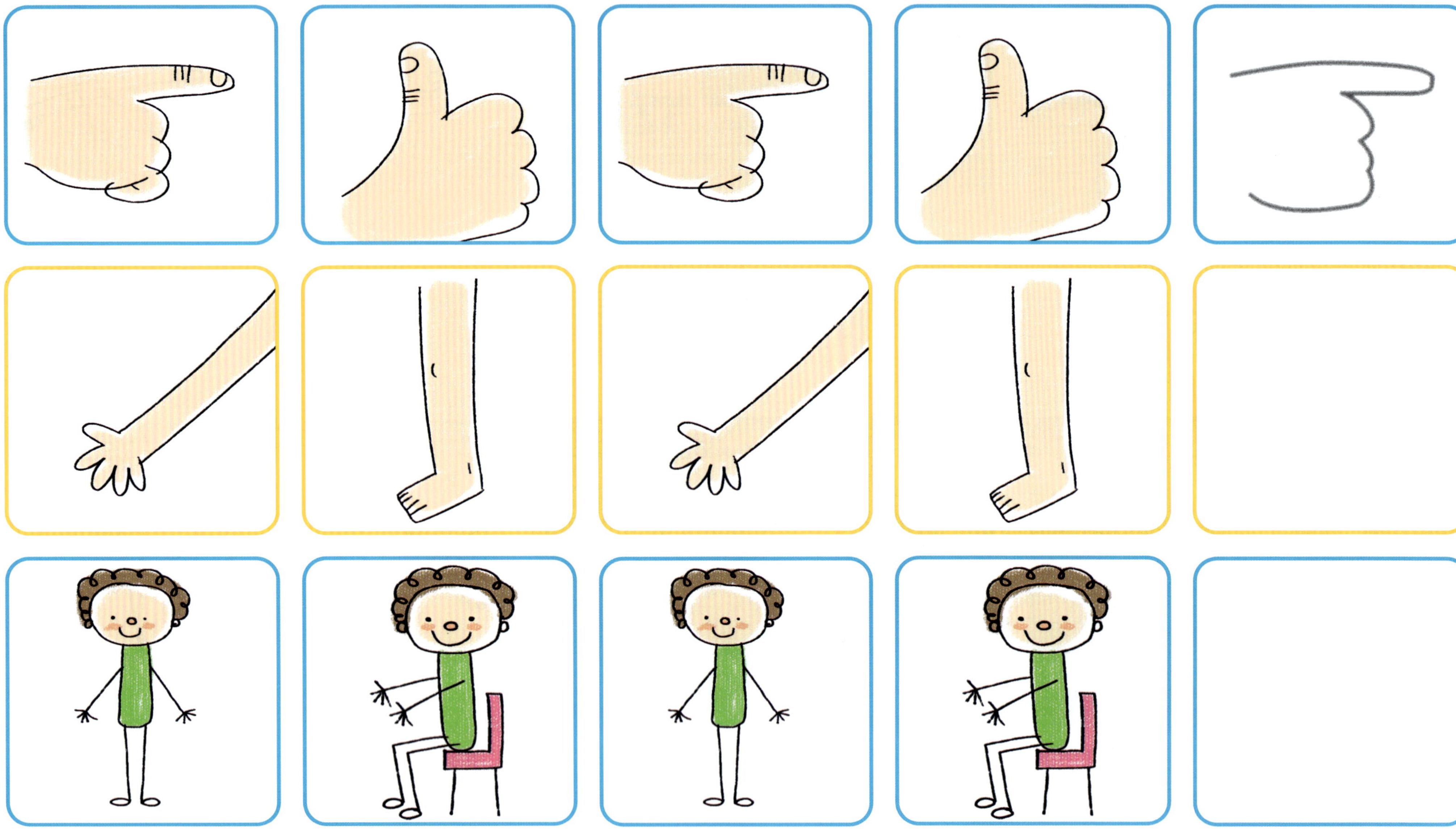

Watch. Listen, point and sing *One finger, one thumb, keep moving*. Draw the next picture in the sequence. Say.

Language: arm, finger, leg, thumb; stand up, sit down, turn round, keep moving

Review

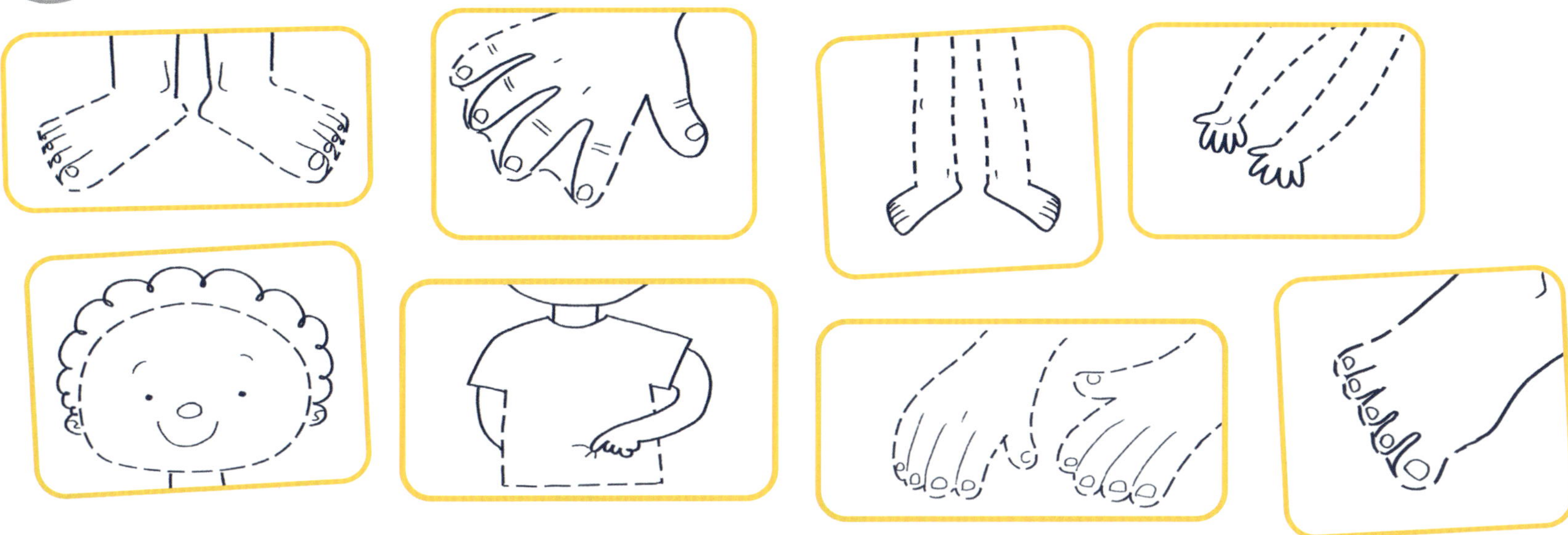

I can …

Vocabulary

Story

Speaking

Content

Trace and color the parts of the body you know. Listen, point and say. Ask and say what you can do. Complete the faces to show what you can do. **Language:** arms, feet, fingers, hands, head, legs, toes, tummy; Can you move your (head)? Yes, I can. / No, I can't. What can you do? I can/can't move my (legs).

Project

Learn a dance. Make a pasta picture of you dancing. Say. Language: arms, feet, fingers, hands, head, legs, toes, tummy; pasta; What can you do? I can move my (arms). I can dance. Can you move your (head)? Yes, I can. / No, I can't. I have (arms). How many (legs) do you have? (Two).

Clothes

Let's dress up!

Listen, point and repeat. Listen and play. Stick the clothes stickers. Circle the clothes Mimi and Dylan are wearing. Say. **Language:** coat, dress, pants, shirt, skirt, sweater; blue, green, orange, pink, red, yellow

2:03 2:04 hello

Listen and find the new clothes. Listen, point and sing *My clothes*. Draw your clothes. Say what you're wearing. Language: pants, shirt, shoes, skirt, socks, sweater; This is my (skirt). These are my (shoes). I'm wearing my (sweater).

Story

2:06

Watch. Listen to the story *Let's dress up!* Circle the clothes Mimi and Dylan wear to the party. Stick the story sticker. **Language:** hat, pants, shirt, shoes, shorts; colors; This is a (shirt). These are (shoes). I'm wearing (a white) (hat).

Story Song

Watch. Listen, point and sing *Let's wear funny clothes today!* Find and circle the clothes Mimi and Dylan wear to the party. Point and say. **Language:** hat, pants, shirt, shoes, shorts, skirt, socks, sweater; colors; (green and brown) (shorts); a (white) (hat)

Speaking

Life skills

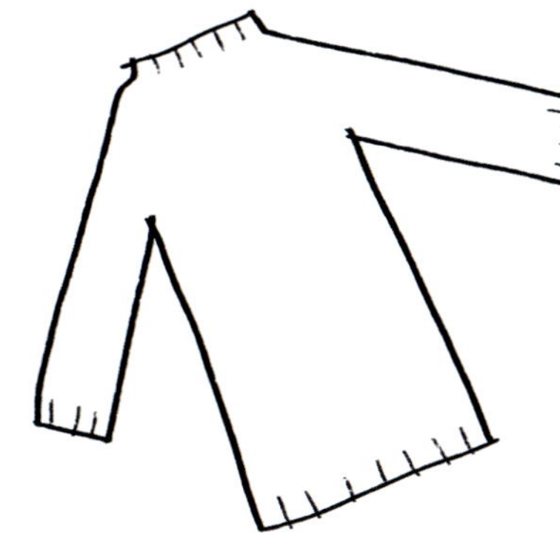

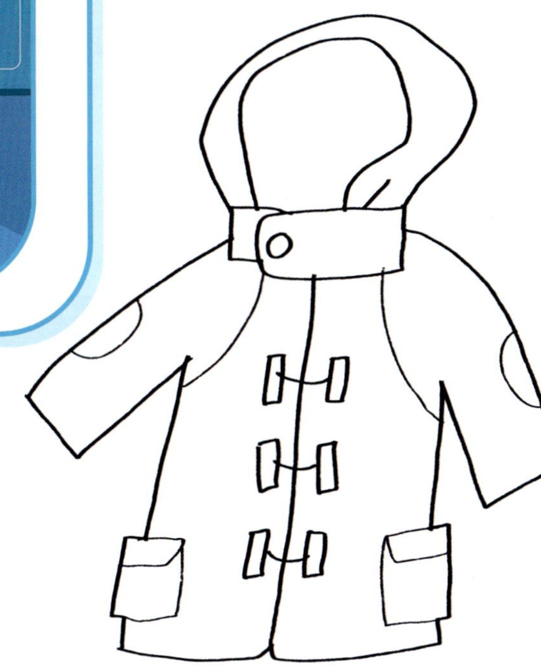

Watch. Listen and point. Match and color the clothes Uncle Dan is wearing. Circle the clothes you're wearing. Say. **Language:** boots, coat, hat, pants, shirt, shoes, sweater; colors; What are you wearing? I'm wearing (a red) (sweater).

2:10

hello

Listen, point and sing *When we play together*. Complete the faces to show if you cooperate with others like Mimi and Dylan. Draw a picture to show you cooperating with your friends or family. Say. **Language:** learn, play, share; family, friends; I (play) with my (friends).

SOCIAL AND EMOTIONAL LEARNING

Content

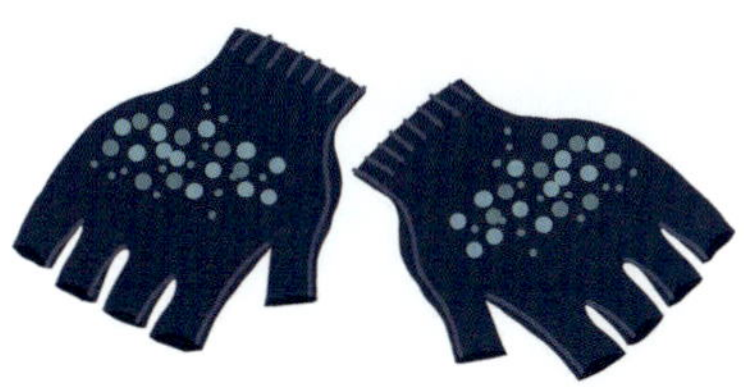

Listen and point. Circle clothes for hot weather orange. Circle clothes for cold weather blue. Say. **Language:** boots, coat, gloves, hat, sandals, scarf, shorts, shirt; cold, hot; It's (cold). I'm wearing (a scarf).

Culture

Watch. Listen, point and sing *This is the way I put on my shirt*. Match the photos and clothes. Say. **Language:** coat, pants, shirt, shoes; This is the way I put on my (shoes).

Review

I can ...

Vocabulary

Story

Speaking

Content

Trace and color the clothes you know. Listen, point and say. Ask and say. Complete the faces to show what you can do. **Language:** coat, dress, gloves, pants, sandals, scarf, shirt, shoes, shorts, skirt, socks, sweater; colors; What are you wearing? I'm wearing (a blue) (skirt).

Project

COOPERATIVE LEARNING

1

2

3

Make a shirt for hot weather or a sweater for cold weather. Hang your clothes on the correct clothes line. Say.

Language: shirt, sweater; clothespin, clothes line, stamps, string; colors; numbers; cold, hot; It's (hot). This is a (blue) (shirt). I like the (green) (shirt). How many (pink) (shirts)? (Two). I have a (blue and green) (sweater). Our clothes are (fantastic)!

Home
Hide and seek

Listen, point and repeat. Listen and play. Stick the home stickers. Circle your favorite place at home. Say. **Language:** bathroom, bedroom, dining room, house, kitchen, living room; blue, green, orange, pink, red, yellow

Listen and find the new places. Listen, point and sing *Where's Sam?* Match Sam and Anna to the places. Color. Ask and say. Language: bathroom, bedroom, garage, house, kitchen, living room, yard; Is Anna in the (yard)? Yes. / No. Where's Sam? In the (yard).

Watch. Listen to the story *Hide and seek*. Circle where Dylan is hiding. Stick the story sticker. **Language:** bathroom, bedroom, dining room, garage, kitchen, living room, yard; Is Dylan in the (kitchen)? Yes, he is. / No, he isn't.

Story Song

1 2 3 4

Watch. Listen, point and sing *Hide and seek is lots of fun*. Trace the numbers. Match to order the pictures. Ask and say. Language: bedroom, dining room, kitchen, living room; numbers 1–4; Is Dylan in the (kitchen)? Yes, he is. / No, he isn't. Where's Dylan? In the (bedroom).

Lesson 5 Speaking

Life skills

Home

Watch. Listen and point. Check (✓) where Kitty and Bruno are. Draw Kitty and Bruno in your favorite place in your house. Ask and say. **Language:** garage, house, yard; cat, dog; Is he/she in the (house)? Yes, he/she is. / No, he/she isn't; He's/She's in the (house). He/She isn't in the (garage).

Values Families are different

Listen, point and sing *Some families are big*. Name the family members in the pictures. Draw a picture of you and your family. Say. Language: family, mommy, daddy, brother, sister, baby, grandma, grandpa; big, small; My family is (small). I have (one brother).

2:23

hello

SOCIAL AND EMOTIONAL LEARNING

Lesson 7 Content

Home

Listen and point. Match the things to the places. Circle the things you put away at home. Say. **Language:** box, closet, shelf, recycling bin; books, clothes, paper, toys; I put (paper) in the (recycling bin).

Home

Watch. Listen, point and say *Round and round the garden*. Trace the numbers. Say the places. Trace and color your favorite teddy bear. **Language:** teddy bear; bedroom, garden, kitchen, living room; Round and round the (garden).

I can …

Vocabulary

Story

Speaking

Content

Color the places you know. Listen, point and say. Ask and say. Complete the faces to show what you can do. Language: bathroom, bedroom, dining room, garage, house, kitchen, living room, yard; Where's (Mimi)? He's/She's in the (bedroom). He/She isn't in the (yard).

Project

Home

Make a house. Put your houses together to make a street. Say. Language: door, house, street, window; carton; colors; numbers; big, small; This is my (house). It's big/small. It's (red). Here's the (window). It's (blue). I have a (red) (house). I like the (yellow) (door). How many (windows)? (Four). Our street is (fantastic)!

Food

I like ice cream!

Listen, point and repeat. Listen and play. Stick the food stickers. Circle the food you like. Say. **Language:** apples, bread, cereal, eggs, ice cream, milk; blue, green, orange, pink, red, yellow

Listen and find the new food. Listen, point and sing *Yummy, yummy*. Match the food to Sam and Anna. Say what you like and don't like. **Language:** apples, bananas, bread, carrots, cereal, eggs, ice cream, milk; I like (carrots). I don't like (cereal). How about you?

Watch. Listen to the story *I like ice cream!* Circle Dylan's favorite food. Stick the story sticker. Language: apples, bananas, carrots, cereal, eggs, ice cream, milk; Put the (eggs) in the cart. I like (ice cream).

Story Song

Watch. Listen, point and sing *The shopping song*. Color the food they buy. Say.
Language: apples, bananas, carrots, cereal, eggs, ice cream, milk; colors; Put the (apples) in the cart.

Watch. Listen and point. Match the food. Circle the food Uncle Dan likes. Color the food you like. Ask and say. **Language:** apples, bananas, bread, carrots, cereal, eggs, ice cream, milk; I like (milk). I don't like (cereal). Do you like (bananas)? Yes, I do. / No, I don't.

Values Helping others

2:36

hello

Listen, point and sing *Little helper*. Color the frames of the people you help. Draw a picture of you helping someone. Say.
Language: mommy, daddy, brother, friend, teacher; I help my (mommy).

SOCIAL AND EMOTIONAL LEARNING

Content

Listen and point. Color the circles green to show food that grows in the garden. Ask and say the food you like and don't like. **Language:** apples, bananas, bread, carrots, eggs, milk, pears, peas, potatoes, tomatoes; I like (potatoes). I don't like (tomatoes). Do you like (carrots)? Yes, I do. / No, I don't.

Food

Watch. Listen, point and sing *Peas pudding hot*. Match the pictures that are the same. Draw a picture of you eating a vegetable you like. Say. Language: peas, pudding, plate, hot, cold; I like (carrots).

I can …

Vocabulary

Story

Speaking

Content

Trace and color the food you know. Listen, point and say. Ask and say. Complete the faces to show what you can do. Language: apples, bananas, bread, carrots, cereal, eggs, ice cream, milk; I like (eggs). I don't like (apples). How about you? Do you like (carrots)? Yes, I do. / No, I don't.

Project

COOPERATIVE LEARNING

Make a plate of food you like. Display your plate of food. Ask and say. Language: apples, bananas, bread, carrots, cereal, eggs, ice cream, milk; modeling clay; I like (eggs). I don't like (apples). Do you like (carrots)? Yes, I do. / No, I don't. I have (bananas). How many (apples)? I can see (four) (eggs). My (ice cream) is (pink). Our food is (fantastic)!

Farm animals

Aunt Emma's farm

Listen, point and repeat. Listen and play. Stick the farm animal stickers. Circle the animals you know. Say.

Language: cow, dog, duck, goat, hen, sheep; blue, green, orange, pink, red, yellow

3:03 3:04 hello

Listen and find the new farm animals. Listen, point and sing *On the farm.* Circle the animals in the song. Point and say.

Language: cow, dog, duck, goat, hen, horse, rooster, sheep; There's a (horse) and a (goat).

3:06

Watch. Listen to the story *Aunt Emma's farm*. Circle the animal that surprises Mimi and Dylan. Stick the story sticker. Language: cow, duck, horse, rooster, sheep; animal noises; There's a (sheep). The (sheep) goes (baa).

Lesson 4

Story Song

Farm animals

Watch. Listen, point and sing *Don't be silly!* Follow and draw the path through the maze in the correct order. Point and say. Language: cow, duck, rooster, sheep; animal noises; There's a (sheep). The (sheep) goes (baa).

3:09

hello

Watch. Listen and point. Match the animals to the photo. Circle your favorite animal. Say. Language: cow, dog, duck, goat, hen, horse, rooster, sheep; There's a (horse). There are (cows).

Values Being kind to animals

Listen, point and sing *Be kind to animals*. Color the people being kind to animals. Draw a picture of you being kind to an animal. Say. Language: cow, dog, duck, goat, hen, horse, rooster, sheep; clean, food, home, kind, water; I like (dogs). I'm kind to animals.

SOCIAL AND EMOTIONAL LEARNING

Content

Farm animals

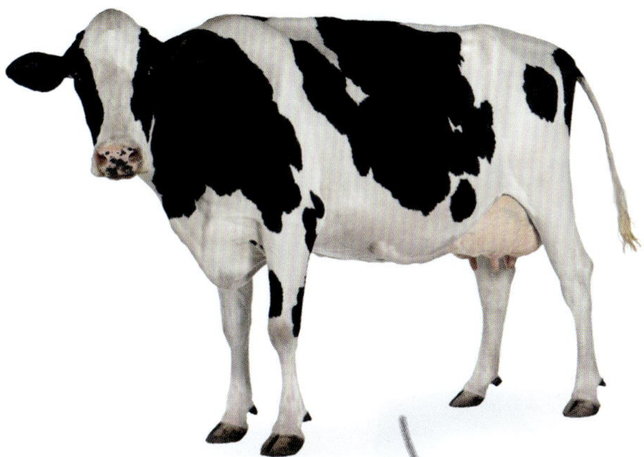

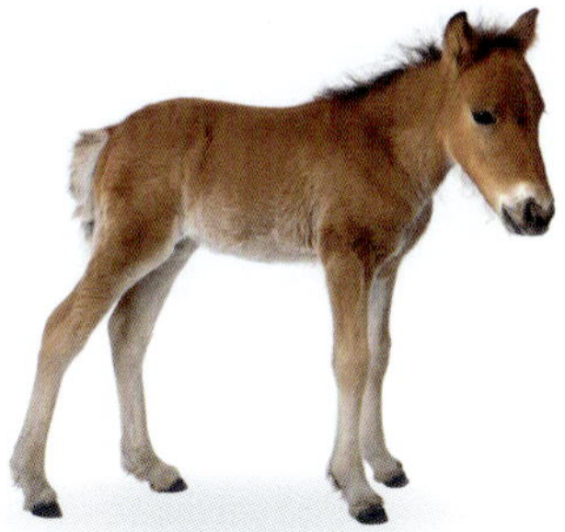

3:11

Listen and point. Match the animals to their babies. Color the star to show your favorite baby animal. Say. Language: cow, calf, dog, puppy, horse, foal, sheep, lamb; This is a (cow). The baby is a (calf).

Lesson 8

Culture

Farm animals

1 2 3 4 5

Watch. Listen, point and sing *Five little ducks*. Color the little ducks.
Trace the numbers. Count the little ducks and circle the correct number. Say.
Language: duck, little, mommy, pond, quack, swimming; numbers; five little ducks

Review

Farm animals

I can ...

Vocabulary

Story

Speaking

Content

Trace and color the farm animals you know. Listen, point and say. Ask and say how many animals there are. Complete the faces to show what you can do. **Language:** cow, dog, duck, goat, hen, horse, rooster, sheep; numbers; There's a (horse). There are (ducks). The sheep goes (baa). How many (hens)? (Three).

Project

COOPERATIVE LEARNING

Make your favorite farm animal. Make a poster of the class's favorite farm animals. Ask and say.
Language: cow, duck, goat, sheep; cotton balls, tissue paper; numbers; colors; There's a (sheep).
There are (six) (ducks). How many (cows)? I like (goats). My (duck) is (yellow). Our farm animals are (fantastic)!

Transportation

Let's go by bike!

Vocabulary Lesson 1

3:14 hello 3:15

Listen, point and repeat. Listen and play. Stick the transportation stickers. Circle the forms of transportation you use. Say. **Language:** bike, boat, bus, car, plane, train; blue, green, orange, pink, red, yellow

Language

3:16 3:17 hello

Listen and find the new transportation. Listen, point and sing *Let's go by boat!* Color the circles green for *yes* and red for *no*. Point and say.

Language: boat, bus, motorcycle, plane, train, truck; Let's go by (bus)! Yes. / No.

Lesson 3 Story

3:19

Watch. Listen to the story *Let's go by bike!* Circle the form of transportation Mimi and Dylan use. Stick the story sticker.

Language: bike, bus, car, train; Let's go by (bike)! I want to go by (car).

Story Song

Transportation

1 2 3 4

Watch. Listen, point and sing *I want to go by bike*. Trace the numbers.
Match to order the pictures. Point and say.
Language: bike, bus, car, train; numbers 1–4; I want to go by (bike). Let's go by (car)!

Watch. Listen and point. Circle the form of transportation that Uncle Dan, Sam and Anna use to go to town. Draw a picture of your favorite form of transportation. Ask and say. Language: bike, bus, car; Let's go by (car)! I want to go by (bike). Do you want to go by (bus)? Yes, I do. / No, I don't.

Lesson 6 Values Thinking of others

3:23

hello

Listen, point and sing *I think of my mommy*. Color the frames of the people you think of. Say. **Language:** mommy, daddy, brother, sister, grandma, grandpa, friend, teacher; I think of my (daddy). I say please/sorry/thank you.

SOCIAL AND EMOTIONAL LEARNING

Content

Transportation

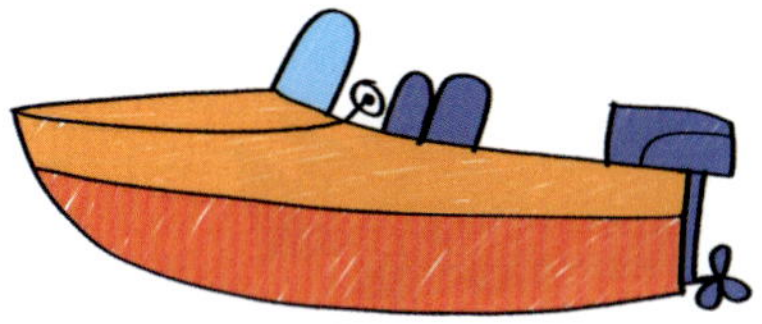

Listen and point. Match the forms of transportation to the places. Say. **Language:** air, road, track, water; bike, boat, bus, car, motorcycle, plane, train, truck; A (bus) goes (on the road). A (plane) goes (in the air).

Lesson 8

Culture

Transportation

3:25

Watch. Listen, point and sing *Row, row, row your boat*. Draw a line to follow the stream. Draw a picture of you in the boat. Say.

Language: boat, dream, row, stream; Row, row, row your boat.

Review

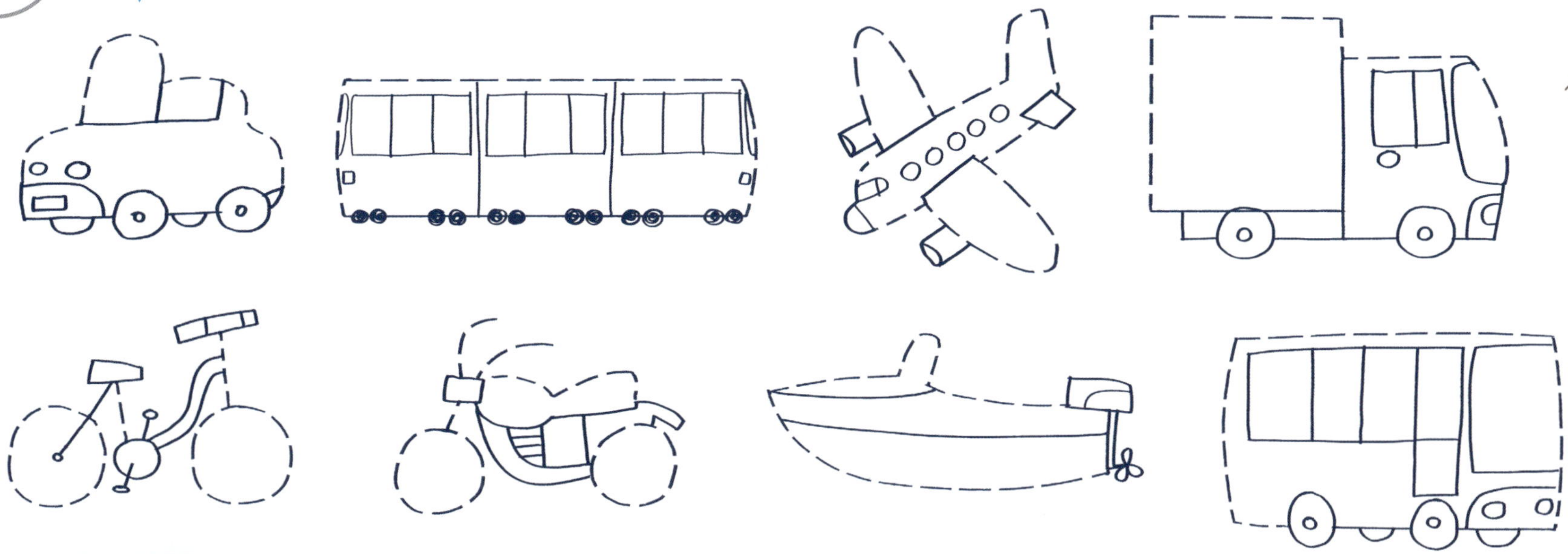

I can …

Vocabulary

Story

Speaking

Content

Trace and color the forms of transportation you know. Listen, point and say. Ask and say which forms of transportation you want to use. Complete the faces to show what you can do. Language: bike, boat, bus, car, motorcycle, plane, train, truck; Let's go by (car)! I want to go by (bike). Do you want to go by (train)? Yes. / No.

Project

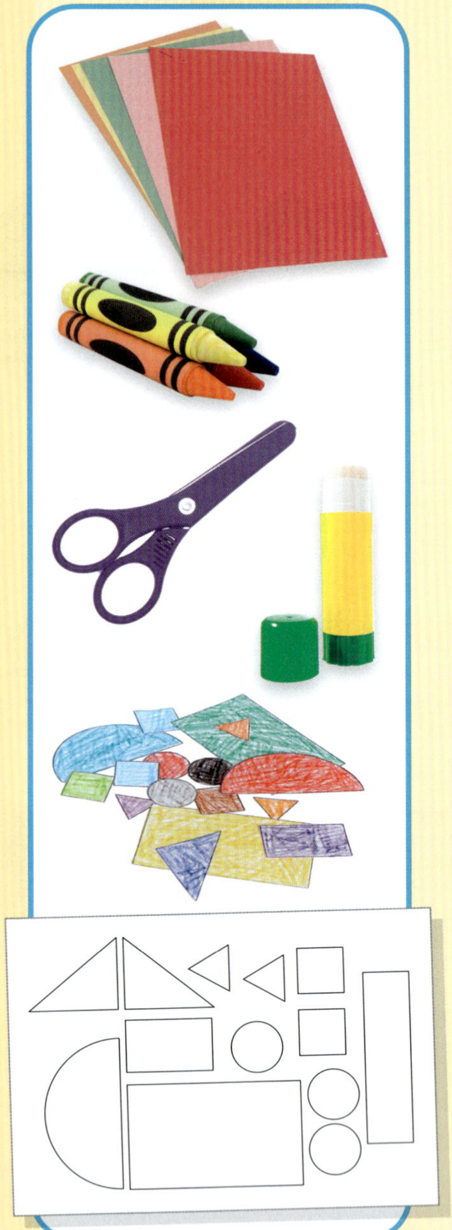

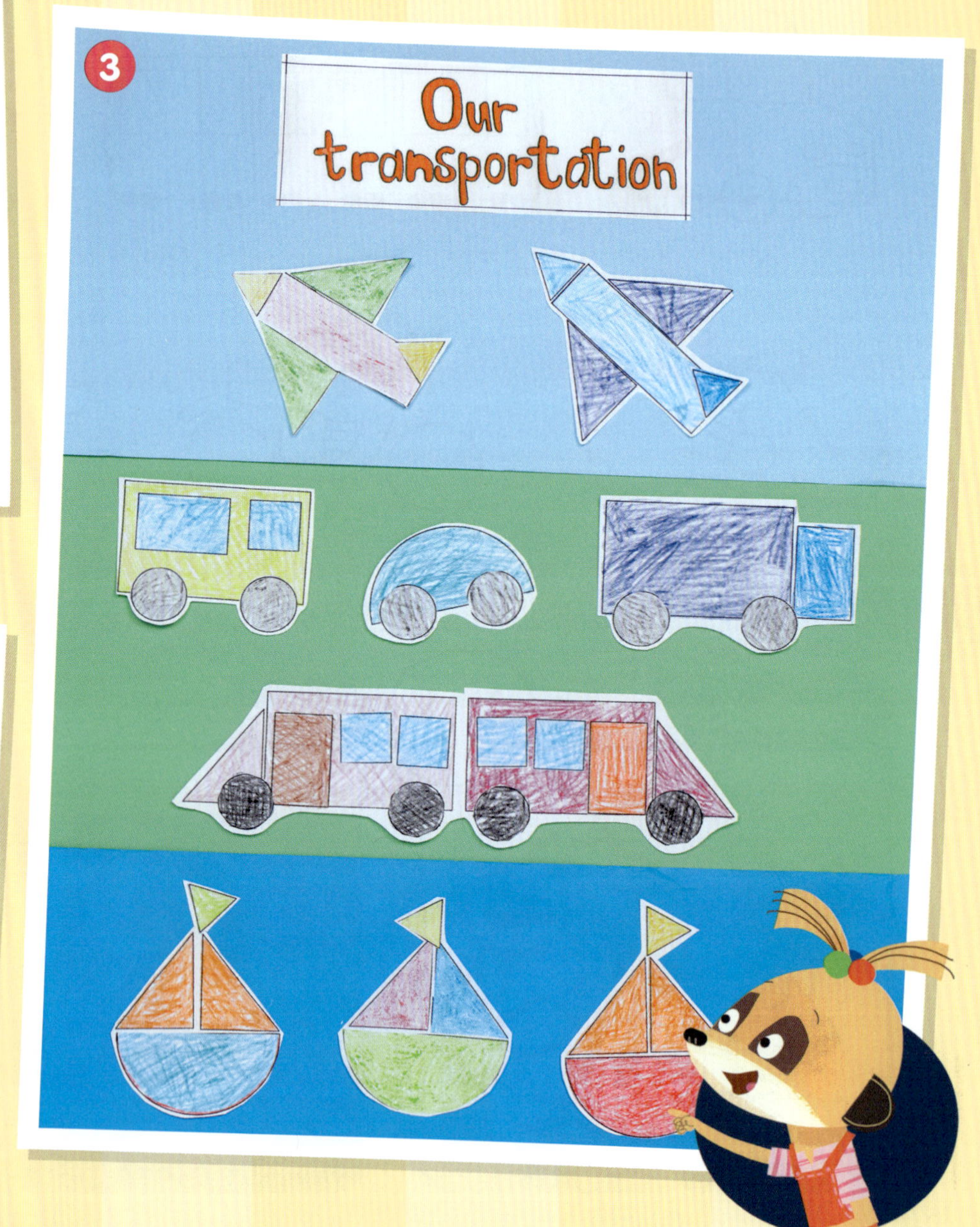

Make different forms of transportation from paper shapes. Make a poster to show the transportation that goes on land, water and in the air. Say. Language: bike, boat, bus, car, motorcycle, plane, train, truck; air, road, track, water; card, paper shapes, scissors; colors; numbers; A (car) goes (on the road). This is my (truck). It's (red). How many (planes)? (Two).

Space

Mimi's dream

Listen, point and repeat. Listen and play. Stick the space stickers. Circle where we live. Say. Language: Earth, moon, planet, sky, star, sun; blue, green, orange, pink, red, yellow

Language

Space

Listen and find the new things in space. Listen, point and sing *What's this?* Match the pictures. Color. Ask and say.

Language: astronaut, moon, planet, rocket, star, sun; What's this? It's (the sun).

Watch. Listen to the story *Mimi's dream*. Circle where Mimi, Dylan and Teddy go. Stick the story sticker. Language: astronaut, Earth, moon, planet, rocket, star, sun; What's this? It's (a planet). Can you see (the moon)? Yes, I can. / No, I can't.

Lesson 4

Story Song

Space

1 2 3 4

Watch. Listen, point and sing *Rocket to the moon*. Trace the numbers. Match to order the pictures. Ask and say. Language: Earth, moon, planet, star, teddy; I can/can't see (the moon). Can you see (a star)? Yes, I can. / No, I can't.

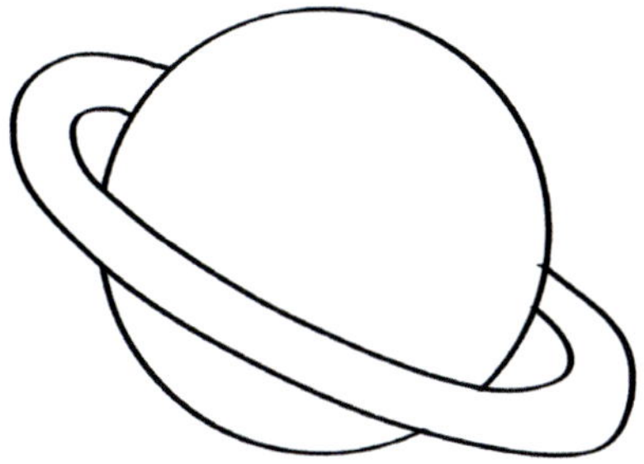

Watch. Listen and point. Match and color the things in space. Count. Ask and say.
Language: Earth, moon, planet, star, sun; numbers; What's this? It's (a planet). Can you see (planets)? Yes, I can. / No, I can't. What can you see? I can see (the stars). How many (stars) can you see?

Listen, point and sing *Sometimes I'm happy*. Color the circles to show the feelings you sometimes have. Draw and color a face to show how you feel now. Say.
Language: angry, calm, happy, sad, scared, sleepy; colors; Sometimes I'm (sleepy).

SOCIAL AND EMOTIONAL LEARNING

Content

Listen and point. Circle the things you can see in the day blue. Circle the things you can see at night black. Say. **Language:** day, night; clouds, moon, rainbow, sky, stars, sun; In the day, I can see (clouds). At night, I can see (stars).

Lesson 8 Culture

Watch. Listen, point and say *Hey diddle, diddle*. Color the characters in the rhyme. Circle your favorite character. Say.

Language: cat, cow, dish, dog, moon, spoon; My favorite character is the (cow).

I can …

Vocabulary

Story

Speaking

Content

Color the things in space you know. Listen, point and say. Ask and say. Complete the faces to show what you can do. **Language:** astronaut, Earth, moon, planet, rocket, sky, star, sun; What's this? It's (a star). Can you see (the moon)? Yes, I can. / No, I can't. What can you see? I can see (the moon).

Project

COOPERATIVE LEARNING

1

2

3

Make a space rocket. Act out a journey to space. Make a class display. Ask and say. Language: astronaut, Earth, moon, planet, rocket, sky, star, sun; toilet roll, stickers; colors; numbers; My rocket is (blue). What's this? It's (a rocket). Can you see (the sun)? Yes, I can. / No, I can't. What can you see? I can see (a planet). I like (the stars).

Colors

Listen, point and say. Match and color the balloons.
Color the star to show your favorite color. Say.
Language: blue, brown, orange, pink, purple

Colors

Listen, point and say. Color the picture following the key. Say your favorite color.
Language: black, green, red, white, yellow

Numbers 123

One to twenty

3:42

Listen, point and say. Draw a line to join the numbers in sequence. Say.
Language: numbers 1–20

Numbers 123

One to twenty

1 2 3 4 5 6 7 8 9 10

11 12 13 14 15 16 17 18 19 20

Listen, point and say. Trace the numbers. Count the balls and circle the correct number.
Language: numbers 1–20

Shapes

Listen, point and say. Trace the shapes in the picture. Say.
Language: circle, oval, star, triangle

Shapes

3:44 hello

Listen, point and say. Match the presents which are the same. Say.
Language: diamond, rectangle, square

Concepts

Listen, point and say. Find and circle four differences in the pictures to show hot and cold. Say.
Language: hot, cold

Concepts

Listen, point and say. Circle the noisy children red. Circle the quiet children blue. Say.
Language: noisy, quiet

Concepts

Listen, point and say. Color the frames of the clean rooms. Say.
Language: clean, messy

Peace Day

Listen and point. Listen and sing *We love the world*. Trace and color the bird of peace. Say.
Language: animals, bird, children, fly, happy, peace, world

Festivals

Carnival

Listen and point. Listen and sing *It's Carnival today*. Match and color the pictures. Color the circle to show your Carnival costume. Say.
Language: Carnival, clown, crown, king, pirate, queen; happy; I'm a (pirate).

Festivals

Children's Day

Listen and point. Listen and sing *It's Children's Day*. Color the frames of the things you love to do. Draw a picture of you doing something you love. Say.

Language: children; hug, play, run, talk; I love to (play).

Hello

Classroom

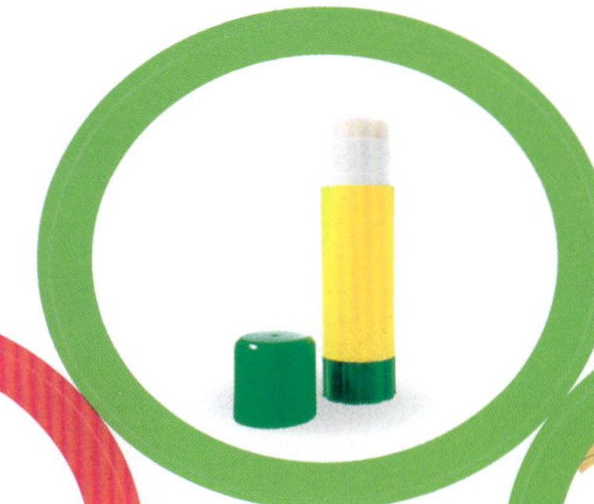

My body

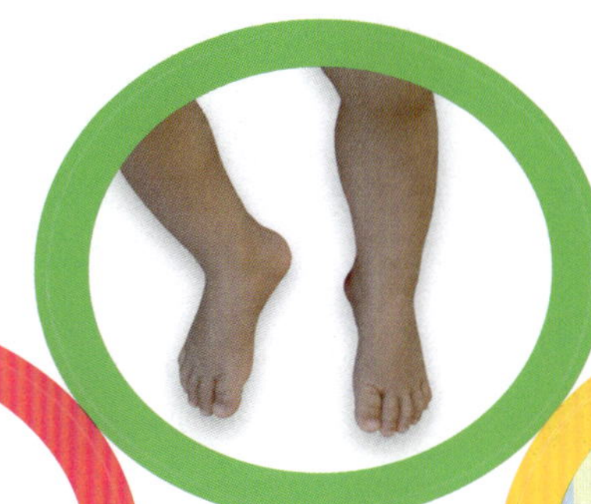

Clothes

Home

Food

Farm animals

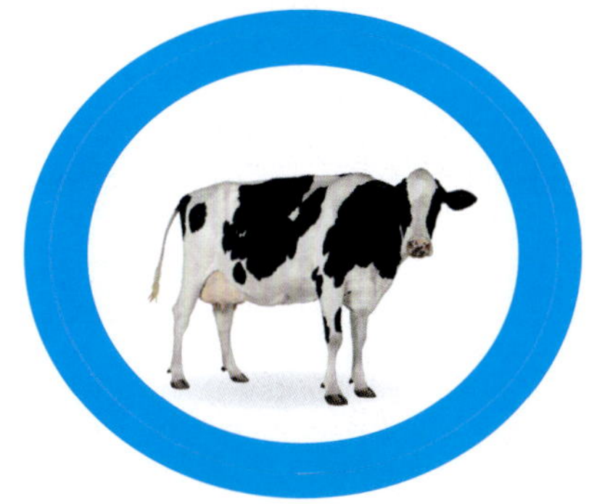

Transportation

Space

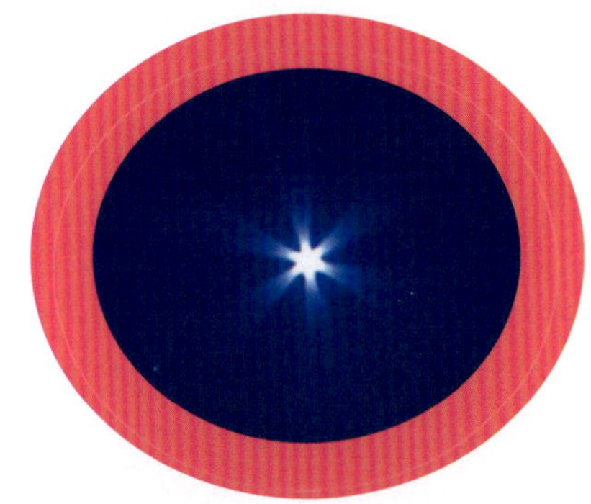